CHINA

SMITHMARK

Text by
Alberto Zola

Graphic design
Anna Galliani

Map
Arabella Lazzarin

Translation
Antony Shugaar and Ann Ghiringhelli

Contents

1 *Beijing is the city of power, symbolized first and foremost by the "Forbidden City", the capital's famous imperial quarter. This bronze lion standing before the Gate of Heavenly Purity is the protector of the "Son of Heaven".*

2-3 *The Palace of Supreme Harmony, the largest structure in the entire "Forbidden City", is 92 feet high, 167 long and 98 wide. In one of the halls emperors of China received and entertained their guests: the most important celebrations were held here.*

4-5 *The Palace of Heavenly Purity was one of the private dwellings of the emperors. During the Ming dynasty the imperial bedchambers were in this building; the throne and writing-desk of the emperor are at the center of this reception room.*

6-7 *The countryside near Gullin in southern China, with its scenic terrain, is scattered with tiny villages surrounded by fertile fields.*

8 *The Peking Opera is an age-old art form, much loved by the Chinese; its traditional characteristics are elaborate costumes, gaudily colored masks, conventional symbolic postures and solemn recitation.*

9 *Confucius, the great philosopher of ancient China, was born in Qu Fu, a small village in the present province of Shandong: this sculpture in stone by the gate of Confucius' house is one of the most visited monuments in China.*

12-13 *Nanjing Lu (Nanking Road) is the most important shopping street in Shanghai and probably in the whole of China: it is lined with the best stores in the country.*

14-15 *A beautiful acrobat shows off her skills in an exercise that looks almost impossible; the main element of its appeal is the elegance and harmony of the forms created.*

16-17 *The Great Wall of China, one of the most amazing construction works in the history of mankind, was built in 225 BC in the north of the country to keep out the barbarian races of Mongolia and Central Asia; it is 7,892 miles long and has an average height of 23 to 26 feet.*

This edition published in 1995 by SMITHMARK Publishers Inc., 16 East 32nd Street, New York, NY 10016.

SMITHMARK books are available for bulk purchase for sales promotion and premium use. For details write or call the manager of special sales, SMITHMARK Publishers Inc. 16 East 32nd Street, New York, NY 10016; (212) 532-6600.

First published by Edizioni White Star. Title of the original edition: Cina, Terra di Millenaria cultura.

ISBN 0-8317-1575-8

Printed in Singapore by Tien Wah Press.

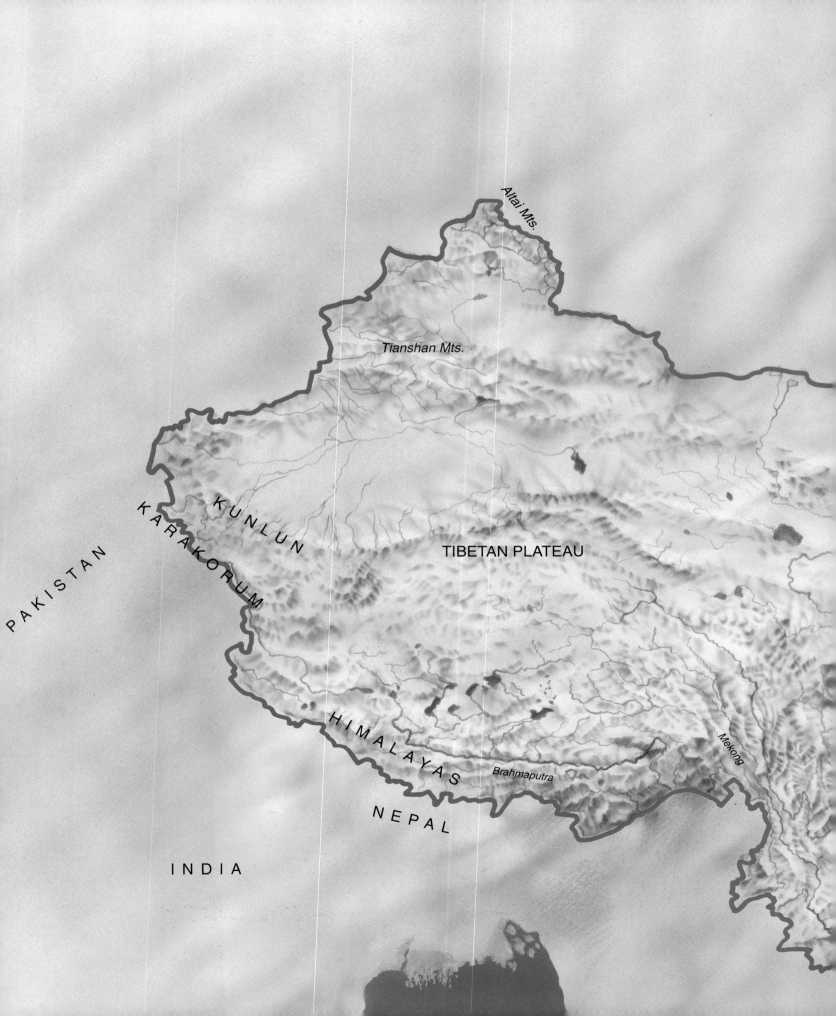

Introduction

The long history of the Chinese empire is marked by an almost total absence of changes in both the social structure and the political superstructure. A ruling class formed of dignitaries and great landholders, led by the Celestial Emperor, governed an enormous number of peasants for this entire span of time. The foundation of political sway was based on economic power, constituted by the control of all agriculture, and on culture, which consisted of a thorough knowledge of the teachings of Confucius — the great philosopher who lived bewteen 551 and 479 B.C. — and the Confucian classics.

At the peak of its development, the Chinese bureaucratic class built an immense empire, equipping it with an economy, a culture, and a written language. The fundamental factor in giving the country a solid agrarian economy was the control of water, without which, given the geographic conditions of China, its climate, and the prevailing characteristics of rice-farming at the time, agricultural production would never have sufficed, so that the flourishing Chinese culture would never have existed. The historical credit which can be claimed by this class of men of letters and dignitaries is that of having fully grasped the importance of this factor, and of having reserved to the state the task of building canals for irrigation and for the transportation of victuals and agricultural products to market, along with tributes and taxes, as well as the construction of reservoirs, dredging operations, and flood-control measures. The construction of these colossal public works, the fruit of the labour of millions of Chinese, had a two-fold advantage: on the one hand, it encouraged the development of agriculture, and on the other hand, by facilitating transportation, it made simpler and more rapid the gathering of tributes, which took the form of grain and which was essential to the survival of the governing class, as well as making it easier to keep huge territories under close control.

Given the impossiblity in practical terms of devoting the same degree of attention and care to all the regions of China at the same time, the bureaucratic class concentrated, through the various phases of the history of the Chinese Empire, on certain regions in a special way, promoting development and public works in those regions. The regions that were thus favoured by the authorities were termed by the Chinese historian Qi Chaoting "key economic zones." According to Qi Chaoting, these "key economic zones" indicated the geographic areas in China that were so fertile and

easily accessible as to constitute a sure source of wealth and political power for whoever might control them. There have been four chief "key economic zones" in the history of China: the valley of the Yellow River, the valley of Changjiang (Yangzi), the Szechuan-Yunan region, and the Guangdong-Guangxi region. The Qin (221-206 B.C.) and Han (206 B.C.-A.D. 221) dynasties established their key economic zone in the valley of the Yellow River, and their capital at Xian. Beginning with the Sui and Tang dynasties, the key economic zone gradually shifted to the valley of Changjiang, so that the succeeding dynasties of Song (capital at Hangzhou), Yuan, Ming, and Qing (capital at Beijing) established definitively and permanently their key economic zone in the valley of Changjiang.

During the periods when China was split into factions and regions, with strong rivalry between groups in power — both during the period when those divisions were prompted by invasions of barbarian peoples, and during those periods when they were the result of civil wars, as for example during the period of the Three Reigns and that of the Five Dynasties — key economic zones of regional dimensions took on enormous importance, such as the Szechuan-Yunan region, and the Guangdong-Guangxi region. During the Yuan, Ming, and Qing dynasties, the imperial government expended enormous efforts to create, in the Haihe valley, around the capital of Beijing, a new key economic zone, but those efforts were unsuccessful.

The end of Chinese isolation in 1840, enforced by the western powers, put an end to this process, which had been going on since the third century B.C., and which had distinguished the entire lengthy course of Chinese history, from the first national unification at the hand of the emperor Shi Huangdi of the Qin dynasty, all the way up to the beginning of the rapidly encroaching decadence of the empire (Qing dynasty). The incursions of the western powers on Chinese interests shifted once and for all the relationship between key economic zones and the imperial ruling class, virtually decreeing the loss of importance of the countryside as a political power base — and political power began to depend more and more upon trade, industry, and large coastal cities — as well as sidestepping the Chinese Mandarins, who were first made equals to the Western colonialists, and finally replaced by them entirely.

In 1840, the first Opium War broke out between Great Britain and the Chinese empire, and China was defeated in 1842. The Nanking treaty (1842) forced the Celestial Empire to allow the opening of five ports for foreign trade, as well as handing over Hong Kong to Great Britain. In 1844, the rulers of China were persuaded to sign similar treaties with France and the United States. With these first "unfair treaties," as they were known, and with the growing economic penetration of Westerners into Chinese territory, began the inexorable decline of the old Imperial China.

In 1884 and 1885, France inflicted a new military

18 *Nomad populations of Chinese Central Asia still live in homes like these; throughout its vast territories the People's Republic of China is inhabited by people of many different races and traditions, with some fifty ethnic minorities.*

19 *This picture was taken in the Yunnan province of south-west China, in a Nasi village called Lijiang; at the local market a Nasi woman ponders over the purchase of a cooking utensil.*

defeat upon China, thus obtaining new economic and territorial advantages and concessions. In the treaty that was signed in 1887, France obtained for itself, along the Chinese-Vietnamese border, the opening of the cities of Longzhou and Mengzi to French commerce. In 1885, besides the leading port cities, such as Shanghai, Nanking, Xiamen, Canton, and Fuzhou, there were a great number of lesser cities open to western trade. Here foreigners had gradually obtained progressively greater privileges: ranging from the right to establish residence and carry on trade all the way up to the right to establish private quarters, and even to pry them from the unwilling Chinese authorities.

The final blow to Chinese sovereignty came nonetheless with the defeat by Japan in the war between the two great empires in Asia in 1894 and 1895. Indeed, this defeat triggered the division of the Chinese territory into "spheres of influence," which were entrusted to the control of the colonial powers, marking the end of the old imperial rule, though this end came officially only a few years later, in 1912, with the foundation of the Republic of China.

Beginning in 1912, the Chinese people fought a long hard battle for its own liberty and to restore Chinese independence. This was a long and painful process, which involved a terrible civil war, and another war with China's old enemy, Japan, ending with the proclamation of the People's Republic of China on 1 October 1949, and with the promulgation of the new Constitution. Over recent years the progress of the young People's Republic in all areas, ranging from economics to scientific research, from health to education and art, has been substantial, but the greatest credit which can be accorded to the ruling class, once drought, crop failures, and mass starvation had been conquered — plights that still afflict many undeveloped nations today — is certainly that of providing the 1.2 billion Chinese all that is needed to live with dignity and self-respect.

One of the most abiding factors of continuity in Chinese history is the form of writing, which took on a strategic value because it had been for many years the exclusive domain of the dignitaries, the powerful caste that held political power. The Chinese language belongs to the Sino-Tibetan language group, and is considered to be one of the most ancient tongues on earth. The earliest surviving written examples of this language date from the early Neolithic (about 4000 B.C.). These are fragments of pottery that bear simple engraved signs that represent, according to the most widely accepted hypotheses, the proper names of aristocratic families.

Before one can really talk about an evolved and mature written language, however, one must wait for the oracular inscriptions, cut into bone and bronze, from the Shang (1751-1122 B.C.) and Chou (1122-221 B.C.) dynasties. There is a close relationship between the fortune-teller's art and the birth of Chinese writing. Ever since the fifth millennium B.C., the Chinese have practised the art of exposing animal bones to the heat of flames, especially the shoulder-blades of cows and turtle shells, and of interpreting the cracking and shattering of the hard materials. According to the Sinologist Vandermeersch, it is fair to say that writing was invented precisely as the diviners took their art to its highest state of technical perfection and symbolic sophistication. Beginning with the Shang dynasty, fortune-tellers began to carve into these bones short phrases, which served to ask specific information of the oracles on occasions such as religious ceremonies, military expeditions, and hunting parties, or in order to receive advice on matrimonial prospects, or information about the outcome of a harvest. This technique was developed and improved throughout the Shang dynasty, and was used right up to the beginning of the Chou dynasty. Parallel with the inscriptions upon the oracular bones, around the end of the Shang dynasty, and more intensely during the Chou dynasty, it became common practice to inscribe upon bronze recipients the proper names of the families as well as more complicated texts.

The language of the inscriptions upon bones and bronzes during the Shang dynasty and at the beginning of the Chou dynasty remained in use until roughly the beginning of the seventh century B.C. This language was replaced by another, used in inscriptions upon bronze, stone, tools, and bamboo during the sixth and fifth centuries B.C., finally culminating in the development of the language of the Classical Chinese Period (last phase of the Chou dynasty), the language found in the texts of Mengzi (Mencio), Zhuangzi, and the other leading philosophers and thinkers of ancient China. The classical Chinese language, which derived directly from the language that was written and spoken between 500 and 200 B.C., found its definitive codification under the rule of the Han dynasty. The written Chinese of modern times is basically the same language that was being written during the Han dynasty. Based on studies done by Scarpari and other contemporary Sinologists, we can safely say that Chinese writing is logographic, although in very loose terms it is often described as ideogrammatic or pictographic.

Every syllable is represented by a character or an ideogram. The ancient Chinese wrote vertically, and from right to left, while nowadays it is customary to write horizontally and from left to right.

The characters used in writing Chinese can be broken down into three categories: simple ideograms, which are those characters that graphically depict abstract ideas and concepts: above, below, good, to love, and so on. Pictograms, on the other hand, portray objects, concrete things, or exceedingly simple concepts. The third category is made up of mixed or composite characters, or characters derived from other characters, such as from the joining of several ideograms or portions of

20 *This beautiful bronze vase is the product of art and craft traditions passed down from one generation to the next over thousands of years, right up to the present day.*

ideograms.

Every character in Chinese corresponds to a syllable, but the number of ideograms is far greater than the number of sounds available. The sum of all Chinese characters that have been used throughout history comes to a grand total of fifty thousand; many of these characters belong to classical tradition, and are no longer used, although the number remains quite high. The number of syllables in the Chinese language is four hundred. To have some idea of how many characters are used to write and speak in everyday modern Chinese, suffice it to consider that newspapers use about six thousand, and children in elementary school learn something like two to three thousand.

For Europeans, it is particularly difficult to learn Chinese because, since it is not an alphabetic language, it has no links with our languages, the number of characters that must be learned is enormous, and those characters have no intuitive link with the respective phonetic units; finally there is the matter of the pronunciation, which involves musical tones, often an insuperable obstacle. The official language in China is the northern dialect, or Mandarin Chinese, which is the language that is spoken in Beijing, but a great many other dialects survive and are used widely, some of them very different from Mandarin. The most important of these other languages is certainly Cantonese, which is spoken in the south of China, and especially in the province of Guangdong, and by most of the Chinese communities outside of China. If the number of languages spoken is huge, there is only one written language, the same for all tongues.

The People's Republic of China extends over an enormous territory of 3.7 million square miles. The vast majority of the population, some 90 or 95 per cent of the total, belong to the Han ethnic groups, but there are more than fifty other ethnic groups present in the People's Republic.

The landscape and climate of this enormous nation encompass a great range and variety: from high mountains to lowlands, from deserts to intensive agriculture, from the icy chill of the Manchurian winters to the tropical heat of the South China Sea. Eighty per cent of the country is mountainous, while the rest — China proper, or at least, the geographic region in which the principal chapters of the history of the Celestial Empire have taken place — extends from west to east, and can in turn be divided into mountainous regions and highlands. The chief highlands are the northwestern highland, the Tibetan plateau (average elevation of thirteen thousand feet), the vast Inner Mongolian tableland, and the Yunnan highlands. There are a great many mountain ranges, but the most impressive ones are surely those running west to east: the chains of the Altai mountains, the Tianshan mountains, the Kunlun, the Qilian, the Karakorum, the Himalayas, the Yinshan, the Qinling, and the

21 top A close-up of the roof of the Palace of Heavenly Purity gives an idea of the work that went into building Beijing's "Forbidden City"; the imperial architects paid meticulous attention to every minute detail.

21 bottom Statues of lions often stand guard over the entrance to the imperial palaces; they are normally in pairs, the male on one side, the female on the other.

22-23 On clear, bright days like this one, the Park of Black Dragon Lake in Lijiang, in Yunnan province, is an even lovelier sight than usual.

Nanling. The great plains areas are the northeastern, or Manchurian plains, which run from Harbin to Shenyang; the northern plains, along the course of the Yellow River, including Henan, Hebei, western Shandong, and northern Anhui, the middle and lower valley of the course of the Changjiang (Yangtse) river, or the provinces of southern Anhui, Jiangsu, northern Zhejiang, northern Jiangxi, the Hubei, and the northern Hunan; the plains of the Zhujiang (the Pearl River), in the southern section of the Guangdong. These level stretches of land occupy a total of one 386,000 square miles, roughly a tenth of the country's total land area.

The immense territory of China spans a broad range of climates. In brief, we can distinguish three main climatic zones: a hot, humid area to the south, which corresponds to the southern provinces that cluster around the city of Canton; a temperate zone in the valley of the Chiangjiang valley, corresponding to the geographic area in which the city of Shanghai is located; and a zone of continental climate, on the plains and hills of the north, where the capital city of Beijing is located.

The capital of the People's Republic of China is a huge metropolis of eight million inhabitants. Chosen as Dadou (Great Capital) for the first time by the emperors of the Mongolian dynasty of the Yuan — the Mongols did not wish to cut off ties entirely with their northern homeland — Beijing was founded as a city of power, and it maintains that structure intact. The chief symbol of that power is certainly the renowned "Forbidden City," which is the imperial quarter, deliberately built separate from the other quarters of the city. Strictly off-limits to the city's populace, and to foreigners, it was conceived in this way by the imperial architects in order to isolate the life of the Celestial Emperor and his court, the very heart of the empire, from the lives of his subjects. It was built between 1407 and 1420, and it underwent various modifications up until the end of the seventeenth century. From 1912 — the year in which the Chinese Republic was first proclaimed — the "Forbidden City" was open to the public, which can finally enjoy a spectacle that has no rivals on earth.

After crossing through the T'ien-an-men (the Gate of Heavenly Peace) and the Duanmen (the Gate of Rectitude), one arrives at the Wumen, or the southern gate; after this gate, one reaches a broad courtyard through which runs the River of the Golden Water (Yellow River), which is crossed by five marble bridges. The principal building that one encounters if one continues straight ahead after passing through the Gate of Supreme Harmony is the Palace of Supreme Harmony, some ninety-two feet in height, one hundred and seventy feet in length, and ninety-eight feet in width, once the site of large and solemn ceremonies. Next comes the Palace of Perfect Harmony and the Palace of the Preservation of Harmony. Here the emperors of the Qing dynasty offered sumptuous banquets to foreign

ambassadors and to their own vassals; here too the much dreaded "metropolitan examinations" were held, for those desiring to rise to the higher levels of administration in the Empire. From here on, one walks past buildings containing the private apartments of the Celestial Emperor and his court.

Among these buildings, we should mention at least the principal ones: the Palace of Celestial Purity, where the emperors of the Ming dynasty had their private residence, the Hall of Union, the Palace of Earthly Tranquillity, residence of the empress during the Ming dynasty, the imperial gardens; the Palace of Spiritual Nourishment, the Six Palaces of the West, the residence of concubines and widowed empresses; the Palace of Abstinence, the Six Palaces of the East; the Hall of the Ancestor Cult, the Palace of Tranquillity and Longevity, established by Qianlong to spend the last years of his life. Inside the palaces, it is possible to admire paintings, calligraphy, sculptures, bronzes, and porcelain of remarkable artistic value. The last gate of the "Forbidden City" is the Beimen, the Northern Gate; if one leaves by this gate, one immediately encounters the Hill of Coal, which looms above the "Forbidden City," and above the Beihai, the imperial lake. The loveliest temple in Beijing is the Heavenly Temple (Tiantan), built in the fifteenth century, and used for centuries by the Chinese emperors as a place of prayer, in which to enter into direct contact with Heaven (Tian), the chief Chinese deity ever since the earliest times. The heart of the modern city is T'ien-an-men Square, one of the largest — if not *the* largest — square in the world, created expressly in the Fifties on the ashes of the old "Tartar city," an agglomeration of small and unassuming low grey houses, inhabited by the populace that was once excluded from the "Forbidden City." In the middle of the square stand the Mausoleum of Mao Zedong and the Monument to the Heroes of the People, while on the two longer sides are the Hall of the People's Assembly and the Museum of Chinese History, which were also built following the Communist revolution. The Museum is divided into four complete sections, plus a fifth section under construction in the nearby Museum of the Revolution. The four complete sections are dedicated to the following topics: the earliest, primitive society (from the origins to 4000 B.C.); the society based on slavery (twenty-first century B.C.- 476 B.C.); the feudal society (475 B.C.- A.D.1840); and the semi-colonial and semi-feudal society (1840-1919).

Shanghai, the city "above the sea," has been a bridge between China and the West for over a century. It was a symbol of foreign colonialism, of ruthless exploitation and vast wealth, of international trade and smuggling, of corruption and vice. For better and for worse, its impetuous and disorderly growth was the result of the progressive occupation of the territory, from the middle of the nineteenth century, until the revolution of 1949, on the part of the Colonial Powers, as the site of industrial activities and international trade. Shanghai has been one of the most active and fertile centres in China, in both cultural and political terms. Here, some of the most important writers in modern China lived and worked, foremost among them Lu Xun; in this city, in 1921, the Chinese Communist Party was founded, the same party that, under the direction of Mao Zedong, brought the revolution to victory.

The process of industrialization of all of China had its beginning in Shanghai and in Manchuria, continuing through the present time. The city of Shanghai is still a leader in the areas of heavy manufacturing, machine tools, textiles, chemicals, and electronics. Shanghai supplies the domestic Chinese market with tools, consumer goods of all sorts (automobiles, bicycles, televisions, radios, cameras, computers, and clothing) and plays a fundamental role in the education and training of technicians who have gone to work in every corner of the great nation. Aside from the industrial activities, this city is the headquarters of the largest stock exchange in the People's Republic of China, and is becoming a financial capital of primary importance. The old section of the city can be split into two distinct areas: the "city of foreign concessions" and the "Chinese city." The "city of concessions" is a large area winding around the port area on the river Huangpu, which in turn runs into the Yangtse, linking Shanghai with the sea.

The two main routes of this area are the Zhongshan Lu or "Bund" — the great boulevard along the river, lined with European-style buildings, once the headquarters of Western banks of all sorts, trading companies, and manufacturers, as well as the foreign legations, now property of the state and the city administration — and the Nanjing Lu, or Nankin Road, the most important trading road of Shanghai. Alongside the former "foreign concessions" lies the "Chinese city," the old section of town, made up of low houses in a labyrinth of alleys teeming with thousands of people. Here one can see the Pavilion of Tea (Wu Xing Ting), located in the centre of a small artificial lake, the Garden of the Mandarin Yu, built in the sixteenth century, and the Temple of the God of the City, which houses interesting statues of Lao-Tse, the founder of the doctrine of Taoism.

Prior to the Opium War, Shanghai was a modest city of fishermen and weavers: today it has become a great metropolis with twelve million inhabitants. Of course, it has taken on not only the size of a great metropolis, but also many of the problems. First and foremost is the traffic, created by thousands of cars, trucks, buses, and bicycles, and the smog that descends upon the city from the industrial zones, concentrated largely around the port.

Canton, located in the fertile delta lowlands of the Zhujiang (Pearl River), is likewise a business and cultural centre of primary importance. It has had a distinct economic and commercial bent for many centuries: under the rule of the Tang dynasty, it

24-25 Although Buddhism originated in India, the religion has been widely practised in China too. This is evident from the hundreds of temples still in existence here, many of them places of worship and pilgrimage for great numbers of believers. The temples seen here are in the vicinity of Kunming, chief city town of Yunnan province: they are the Huating temple (top) and the Gilt Temple (bottom); the Buddha in the foreground (right) is in the Taihua Temple.

became the main trading city between the Chinese Empire and the countries of southeast Asia; between the end of the seventeenth century and the earliest decades of the nineteenth century, it held a virtual monopoly on sea trade and was the headquarters of the leading mercantile corporation; in the middle of the nineteenth century, it was the last city to open communications with the west, and is still one of the foremost destinations of businessmen from all over the world. Today Canton is a large city, with its own Exhibition Hall where many of the largest and most important trade fairs of the Far East are held, as well as a broad array of resources necessary to make it one of the most modern and developed cities in China.

Alongside the new city, Canton maintains its ancient personality. Developed alongside the Zhujiang (Pearl River), Canton is so much in thrall to the river's charm that all of its most important streets run down towards it. In the old town stand some of the oldest Chinese temples that have survived to date: the Temple of the Six Banana Trees (Lui Hongsi), founded in A.D. 479; the Mosque of the Memory of the Saint (Huang Shengsi), not far from this; and the Temple of Guang Xiaosi, which is believed to date back to a period prior to the foundation of the city itself. Likewise, in the heart of the city, is the island of Shamian, the neighbourhood where, during the nineteenth century, the English and French established their "territorial concessions." A number of the phases in the long process of the Chinese revolution took place in this city, which commemorates its history in the museum dedicated to Sun Yatsen, one of the most famous of all Chinese revolutionaries, and in the Revolutionary Museum of the Guangdong. It is impossible to discuss Canton without making some mention of its great tradition of fine food and cooking. The cuisine of Canton is one of the most varied, exquisite, and popular in all of China. It is well known in China, but it is safe to say that in all the largest cities on earth, most Chinese restaurants serve almost exclusively Cantonese dishes.

Beijing, for centuries the sumptuous political capital of the longest-lived empire in history, and now capital of the People's Republic; Shanghai, the driving force of western colonialism and the chief site of trade from and to China and of modern industry; Canton, the first and for many centuries the only port open to western markets and the theatre of the events that led up to the Opium War, which forced the old Celestial Empire to deal with the emerging European industrial powers, are the most representative and best known Chinese cities in the world.

If, when we visit China, we are amazed and fascinated by the remarkable size and beauty of these symbolic cities, we should not forget that outside these cities, now as in centuries past, there is a huge countryside created through the labour of hundreds of millions of silent peasants, the engine of the thousands of years of history of China, the source of power and wealth, a spectacular, grandiose monument to the Chinese civilization.

Beijing, the Temple of Heaven

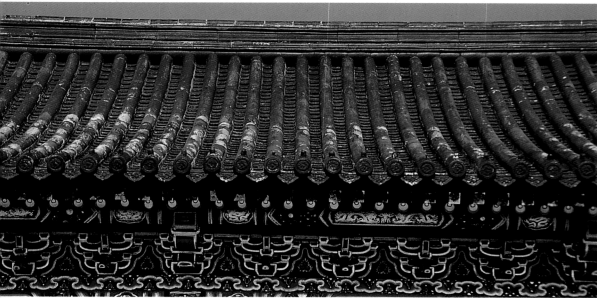

26 top *The Temple of Heaven - "T'ien T'an" to the Chinese - is one of the finest buildings of classical architecture. It stands at the centre of a park with many trees, in the southern part of the city.*

26 bottom *The Temple has a circular layout and its base is formed of three circular floors. The circular concentric roofs, also three in number, give a dignified, elegant line to the structure. The photo highlights a detail of the roof of one of the gates of the temple.*

27 *The Temple of Heaven was built in 1409 by emperors of the Ming dynasty. Although restored in the second half of the 18th century, its original structure remains substantially intact; for centuries it was one of the places of prayer preferred by the "Son of Heaven".*

28-29 *The great expertise of Chinese architects and craftsmen is seen at a supreme level in the Temple of Heaven; it is particularly worth noting the skill with which wooden beams and pillars were wedged into place to support the roof of the "T'ien T'an", and the highly colourful decorative effects created with the brushwork of Chinese artists.*

30 top *The Ming dynasty followed the Mongols of the Yuan Dynasty and ruled the Empire from 1368 to 1644. Under the Mings China lived one of the finest periods of its long history. The statue in the photo is one of the many lying near the Tombs of the Mings, not far from Beijing.*

30 bottom *Monasteries of all the world's main religions are to be found in Beijing. Lamaism too has its places of worship in this huge city.*

31 *Buddhism arrived in China from India, where it originated, in the first century AD but it was a long time before it made any real impact. It spread more rapidly from the 4th century onwards but had to withstand hostility from the imperial "establishment" and also come to terms with the prevailing popular beliefs of the Chinese.*

32-33 *The pagoda is one of the most typical forms of Buddhist architecture. These buildings, which are places of worship, have a typically pyramid-shaped structure with a varying - but always odd - number of storeys and projecting roofs. The oldest pagodas were made entirely of wood.*

From T'ien-an-men Square
to the "Forbidden City"

34 *The Ch'anmen gate, one of the oldest in the city of Beijing, stands on the southern side of T'ien-an-men square, the Square of the Gate of Heavenly Peace. One of the largest in the world, this square has witnessed all the major events that have marked the most triumphant and tragic moments of China's history over the last few decades.*

35 *Standing in T'ien-an-men square, in front of the main entrance to the "Forbidden City", is one of the foremost monuments of modern China, the Monument to the Heroes of the People, together with the Mausoleum of Mao Zedong, the People's Assembly Building and the Museum of Chinese History. The square has become a significant symbol of China's new political power structure.*

36-37 *Beyond the Wumen, the southern gate of the "Forbidden City", the River of Golden Water flows through a spacious courtyard. Here we see, in the foreground, the five marble bridges which cross the river; in the background, the Gate of Supreme Harmony.*

37 *This is the best known view of Beijing, all over the world: T'ien-an-men, the Gate of Heavenly Peace. Across the square is the Southern Gateway.*

38 top *Close to large buildings and vast courtyards there are also smaller spaces and narrow passageways, like this side alley leading to a secondary gate of the "Forbidden City".*

38 bottom *To the north of the "Forbidden City" the so-called Hill of Coal overlooks the entire imperial quarter. Visitors who climb to its top are greeted by this unforgettable spectacle.*

39 top *The Hall of Mutual Prosperity, or Jiaotai Dian, is situated between the Palace of Heavenly Purity, home of the emperor, and the Palace of Earthly Tranquillity, residence of the empress. Between the two the Hall of Mutual Prosperity represents the union of the venerable couple.*

39 bottom *Tourists can reach the Palace of Supreme Harmony taking one of the white marble bridges over the River of Golden Water; on the other side is a series of spacious courtyards and imposing buildings.*

40 left *This bronze statue depicting a graceful heron is in front of the Hall of the Conservation of Elegance which, at the end of the last century, was the private apartment of Emperor Ching Ti. The heron is a symbol of long life.*

40 top right *As well as its prestigious buildings, private dwellings, courtyards and gateways, the "Forbidden City" contains an abundance of objects, large and small, used to decorate both its interiors and exteriors; here we see a tripod, formed from a pair of swans cast in bronze.*

40 bottom right *The emperors particularly liked bronze or marble statues of elephants and turtles since these creatures were symbols of power and longevity.*

41　*To the Chinese the turtle has great symbolic value; in antiquity priests used these animals' shells for oracular divination. The very first evidence of Chinese writing stems from the ancient practice of inscribing the oracles' answers on the shoulderbones of cattle and on tortoise shells.*

43 top *A favourite residence of emperors, the Palace of Heavenly Purity is among the most lavishly furnished; close to the throne are precious incense-burners.*

43 bottom *A fine imperial sedan chair can be seen in the Hall of Mutual Prosperity which once also housed the throne of the empress.*

44 left *When the lakes turn to ice in winter they become a huge skating rink; in summer they are crowded with boats and bathers trying to escape from the heat of the city. The photograph shows one of the gateways into the park.*

44 top right *Belhai is a maze of avenues, paths, canals, bridges, pagodas, trees and stones, with a large lake set in their midst, and all entirely man-made. The Fanhshan Fandian (meaning Imperial Restaurant), renowned for its superb Chinese cuisine, is in the centre of this big park.*

44 bottom right *The Clock Tower stands at the very heart of Belhai park which was opened to the public only in 1925 and has been hugely popular ever since; at weekends it is packed with as many as half a million visitors.*

45 *Belhai, the Imperial Park, is full of interesting things to see; the people of Beijing love coming here and it is crowded every single day of the week. In the foreground is one of the pagodas - the Pagoda of the Thousand Years - which help make this park such an unusual place.*

On the Roof of the World

46 top *80% of the landmass of the People's Republic of China is covered by mountains and plateaux, extending mainly from west to east. The Tibetan and Qinghai plateaux are enclosed by border ranges, the Himalayas and the Kunlun Mountains.*

46 bottom *Soaring 29,000 feet above sea level, Everest is the world's highest mountain; part of the Himalayas range, it is situated between Nepal and Tibet.*

47 *At the monastery of Rongbuk, built under the north face of Mount Everest, called "Chomo Lungma" in Tibetan, monks live in isolation, far from the civilized world.*

48-49 *The Himalayas range - viewed from the north in this photo - includes many other peaks reaching between 25,000 and 28,000 feet above sea level.*

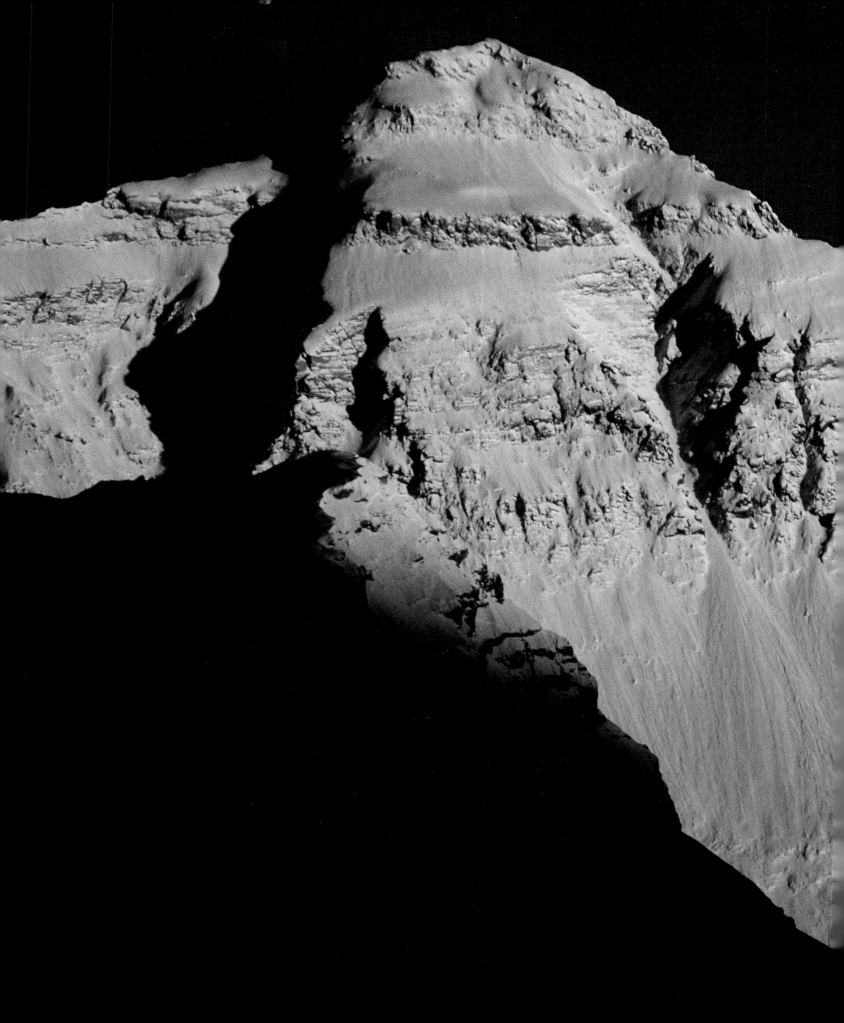

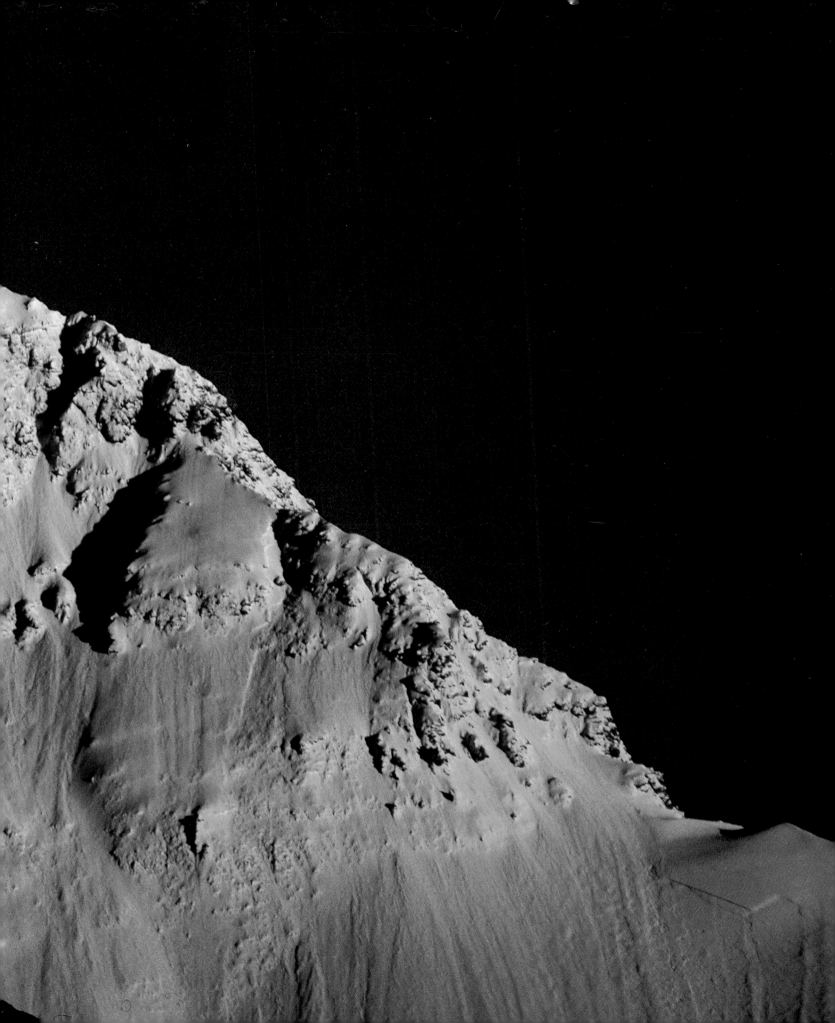

The Regions
of the West

50-51 *Prayer flags blowing in the wind are typical signs of the devout religious practices of the people who inhabit the huge, highland Tibetan Plateau.*

51 *There are few good roads in Tibet and the ones leading to the mountainous regions are particularly treacherous. The journey to Mount Everest involves crossing numerous villages and valleys carved out by rivers of rushing icy water.*

52-53 *Hotan - an old oasis town along the Silk Road in the autonomous Xinjiang region, in the heart of Central Asia - is approached along a wide, tree-lined avenue.*

54 *About 80% of China's population live in rural areas and, in spite of the continuous advances made by industry, agriculture is still the mainstay of China's economy. The farming district shown here is in central Sichuan, one of the most fertile parts of China.*

55 *Chinese territory changes from very fertile areas to barren, hostile highland regions. The only crop grown in Baixi villages is maize, which people leave to dry on their rooftops.*

56-57 *This giant panda is one of the very few to have survived in its natural environment, China's bamboo forests; thanks to the concerted efforts of zoologists and ecologists this creature has been saved from extinction.*

57 *Moving westwards the landscape changes: at Jiuzhalgou, in Sichuan, the scenery is reminiscent of typical alpine regions, with lakes, jagged mountain peaks and pine forests.*

58-59 *The Tibetan Plateau stretches as far as Qinghai province, in western China. Like Tibet, Xinnjiang and Inner Mongolia, Qinghai is a border region where agriculture and livestock-farming are the main activities; peasants live in small villages like the one shown here.*

The Great River

60 top left *From its source in the Tibetan Plateau the Yangtze River travels over 3,728 miles eastward, through deep gorges and big cities, to join the East China Sea near Shanghai.*

60 bottom left *A small craft sails on the great Yantze River, which flows through one of the world's most fertile areas: China's "Key Economic Zone", which is still the mainstay of the country's agricultural system today.*

60 bottom right *The three principal rivers of China are the Yellow River, the Yantze and the River of Pearls. In ancient China a system of interconnected canals which received water from the three rivers, provided a network of navigable waterways and supplied water to the country's outstandingly efficient irrigation system.*

61 *The Yangtze is navigable for over 1,900 miles: this fact, together with the exceptional fertility of the regions it flows through, has made this river China's major "highway". It was by gaining control of the Yangtze that the colonial powers succeeded in extending their authority over such a huge and important geographical area.*

62-63 *The Forest of Stone, in Yunnan province, is one of the strangest sights the Chinese landscape has to offer, a "must" on every tourist itinerary.*

Pasturelands and Steppes

64 top *Bactrian camels are traditionally used by Mongol peoples as a means of transport; typically found in the temperate regions of Central Asia, they stand as high as 8 feet and weigh up to 400 kilos.*

64 bottom *Turpan is an ancient oasis town on the Silk Road, a stopping-place for caravans travelling between the Celestial Empire and western Asia; once an important trade centre, it is now a prominent archaeological site.*

65 top *A group of camels graze in the vast pasturelands of Inner Mongolia. A rare breed of wild camels lives in the Gobi Desert.*

65 bottom *A herd of wild horses drink at a small lake in the steppes of Inner Mongolia. Horses and camels were precious allies of the Mongols during the most glorious periods of their history.*

66-67 *Guangxi is an autonomous region in southern China, on the Vietnamese border: its spectacular landscape is characterized by thousands of tiny plots of land interrupted here and there by great expanses of rocky, eroded hillside.*

68-69 *Cormorants feed on fish and excel both as divers and swimmers; if trained for the purpose, they can be valuable fishing aids.*
This picture - taken near Gullin - shows cormorants being used for night-time river fishing, a common practice in many countries of the Far East.

Descendants of the Celestial Empire

70 top *The dragon is one of the symbols of the Emperor and a recurrent theme of traditional events held during the most important Chinese festivities.*

70 bottom *In spite of the huge conurbations and advanced industrialization of present-day China, agriculture still has strategic importance in the Chinese economy. Here we see a peasant hard at work in the fields near Lijiang, in Yunnan province.*

71 *Every year millions of people from every corner of China flock to the "Forbidden City". In this picture a family in traditional costume poses for a souvenir snapshot in front of one of the main gates of the famous "imperial quarter".*

Accent on Education

72-73 *Literacy is a means of contributing towards the modernization of a country fired by ambitious goals. Well aware of this, the leaders of the People's Republic of China have always* given prominence to the education of the masses. Here we see a group of high-spirited schoolchildren seated on a bench on the Bund, Shanghai's riverside boulevard.*

73 top *A group of Chinese girls with smiling faces and pretty dresses - their teacher behind them - enjoy posing for a souvenir photo during a special celebration at school.*

73 bottom *Until not long ago we were used to seeing Chinese adults and children all wearing the same uniform; now it comes almost as a surprise to note that the wind of change has affected dress as well.*

New fashions and traditional styles

74 Coca-Cola and disco-music have caught on among China's younger generation, in Shanghai as elsewhere. There are discothèques and karaoke-discos in just about every big city.

75 In the last ten years all the myths of Western consumer society have been imported into China, with no exceptions: in the streets of central Beijing, crowds stroll past modern buildings amid the signs of well-known American fast-food chains and hoardings emblazoned with typically Western cult figures.

76-77 One of the thousand specialities offered by Chinese cuisine is served in a restaurant: small pieces of fish, meat, vegetables, noodles and tofu are cooked by dipping them briefly into a pot of water, kept constantly on the boil over a flame. It's been said this speciality resembles the French "Bourguignon".

78-79 *The Chinese are true masters of circus skills. The circus is one of the most popular forms of entertainment in China and performances of the kind shown in these pictures frequently delight audiences in big cities throughout the country. Circus traditions have been passed down through the centuries and there are famous schools where these performers train.*

Peking Opera

80 *After years of difficulties and lack of interest, due mainly to the hostile political climate, the Peking Opera is again in vogue and troupes perform in the country's leading theatres.*

81 *For a long time the schools where Peking Opera performers trained also suffered the consequences of official disapproval; now, with a new lease of life, they take in talented - and increasingly younger - students who see this unique art form as their life-long vocation.*

82 *Much of the Peking Opera repertoire is based on classics; in recent years, while remaining faithful to traditional forms of expression, new versions of these musical verse plays and new interpretations of age-old plays have been introduced.*

83 *Two actors get made-up for the performance: this is an important part of the preparations since make-up and costumes identify the characters of the Peking Opera in a highly stylized way.*

A world whose days are numbered

84 *At the Yungfengsi monastery in Lijiang, in Yunnan province, an old monk poses for the photographer in front of the entrance to the temple. Immediately after the advent of the People's Republic of China, young men caught up in the revolutionary fervour left the monasteries behind them; now, with success and money the new utopia of Chinese youngsters, novices are few and far between.*

84-85 *There are still places in China where time seems to have stood still: in a Ch'iang village, in Sichuan province, these two men use an age-old method to draw wine from a terracotta container.*

The Bay Yinghuo Shao Brigade

86 *The Leader of the Bai Yinghuo Shao Brigade, in the autonomous region of Inner Mongolia, perfects his skills at archery, in this case used more for hunting than for sport.*

87 left *A camel handler of the Bai Yinghuo Shao Brigade takes a short break from his work and poses for a photo. Camels are still one of the most valued forms of transport for the peoples of the Gobi desert or the vast pasturelands of Inner Mongolia.*

87 top right *A handler tends to a camel of the Bactrian breed, with two humps.*

87 bottom right *The single room inside a Mongol tent, heated by a central stove, holds all the family's furnishings. In the photo the cooking and living area can be seen on one side, the sleeping area on the other.*

88 The island of Hainan-tao in the South China Sea, part of Guangdong province, is almost as large as Taiwan. Its inhabitants are practically all fishermen and farmers.

89 The natural beauty of Hainan-tao has made it a popular tourist destination. It can be reached by sea, from Canton and Hong Kong, or by air, thanks to the two airports of Haikou and Sanya.

90-91 The main products of the island are rice, sugar cane and - primarily - fish from the bay of Yalong. Tiny eating-places along the coast serve delicious dishes made with fresh fish and ginger.

Beyond Beijing....

92 top *A lively trade centre, Kunming is most important as a hub for road and rail traffic directed towards South-East Asia. The so-called Green Lake can be seen in this view of the city.*

92 bottom *The river Lui flows through the town of Yang Shon and continues across the autonomous region of Guangxi, close to the border with Vietnam.*

93 *The province of Yunnan has many attractions, including the Forest of Stone and the Three Pagodas National Park. This picture shows the most celebrated pagoda of the three.*

94-95 *The Octagonal Pavilion of the Yuantong Temple is the jewel of Kunming, chief city of Yunnan province. The Yunnan is a vast plateau bordering with Burma, Laos and Vietnam and crossed by the upper reaches of the rivers Mekong and Yantze. Because of its border position, this part of the country has most felt the cultural and religious influences of nearby Indochina.*

96-97 *As a symbol of China the "Great Wall" is famous worldwide. Built as fortification to keep out the "barbarians" of central and southern Asia, it also marked the boundary between Chinese civilization, on the inside of the wall, and the barbarian Hsiung-nu, or Huns, on the outside.*

98 *Hangzhou, ancient capital of the Southern Sung dynasty, is one of China's loveliest cities. So wrote Marco Polo in "Il Milione", the tale of his travels, and his opinion is borne out by the splendour of its many age-old monuments. The Luho Pagoda, shown here, is but one small example.*

98-99 *In the heart of Canton - Guangzhou in Chinese - stands the Palace-museum dedicated to Sun Yat-sen, father and mentor of the Nationalist Revolution of 1911. A man of humble birth, after graduating in medicine, he immediately made politics his full-time activity; he founded China's first modern political party and led many rebellious campaigns until the Ch'ing dynasty was finally brought down in 1911.*

The Terracotta Army

100 *China was the scene of one of the most spectacular archaeological finds of all time, the Terracotta Army of Xian: thousands of life-size terracotta carriages, horses and warriors, the funerary trappings of the Ch'in emperor, Shih Huang Ti.*

101 *Anyone wanting to fully appreciate the true value and significance of ancient Chinese culture should not fail to visit the museum opened in Xian on the site of the sensational discovery. The museum complex includes a restoration workshop and a prestigious research centre.*

Confucius

102-103 *The house, temple and tomb of Confucius are situated at Qu Fu. From the Han dynasty onward Confucian temples began to spread throughout China but his teachings were never regarded as a religion. Even today the Chinese are well aware of the fundamental contribution Confucius made to the creation of the Chinese State.*

Tibet: land of monasteries

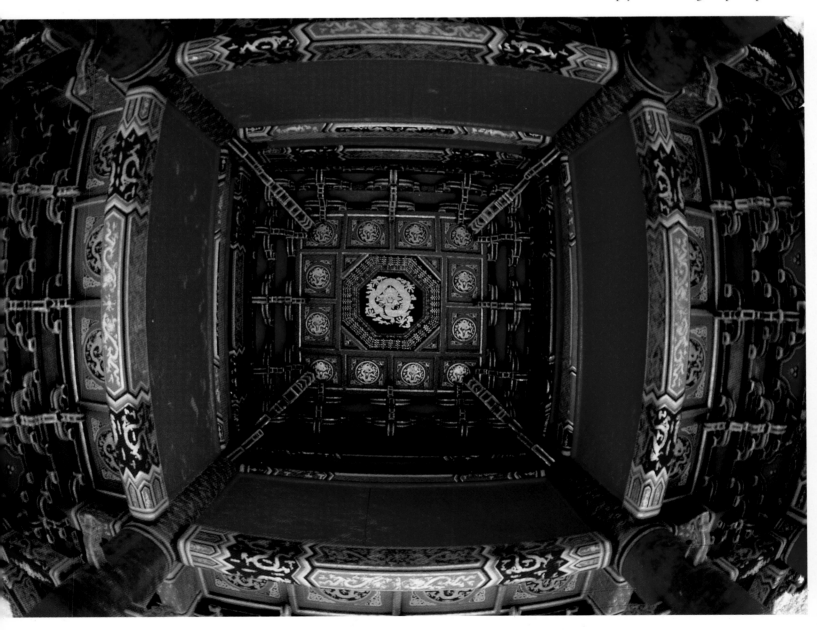

108-109 *Overlooking the city of Lhasa, capital of Tibet, is the imposing Potala Palace. This complex group of buildings, which include temples, living quarters and fortifications, is inhabited by Lamaist monks. It is the most important and best known of the many monasteries in Lhasa, the holy city of Tibetan Buddhists.*

106 *The fascinating temple of Lingyin is in Hangzhou, chief city of Chekiang province. The Qingling-dong grotto was created near here in AD 951: the composition, carved with incredible skill and dedicated to an Amidist Buddha, includes numerous other small Buddhas, just under 50 cm high.*

107 top *At Leshan, in Sichuan province, an enormous statue of Buddha, over 230 feet high, has been carved in the rock; it dates back to 713 AD.*

107 bottom *A wide variety of styles have been employed to venerate Buddha in just about every corner of China: the statues carved out of rock - typically found in southern China - are a magnificent example of religious art.*

The Potala monastery is an enormous size. It contains temples, private dwellings of monks and lodgings for pilgrims, refectories, meeting rooms and halls for seminars and community gatherings - a kind of holy city within a city.

Tibetan art is solely religious and essentially of Indian origin; the earliest examples date back to the time when Buddhism was first introduced into the country. The precious frescos on religious themes seen in this picture further enhance the value of the Potala monastery.

Shanghai: China's Largest City

112 top *Shanghai may be a modern, westernized city but there is still plenty of evidence of oriental cultures and religions, for instance this statue of Buddha in Longhua temple.*

112 bottom *The port on the Huang-p'u river is the most important in China and one of the world's largest industrial areas has grown up behind its waterfront (starting from the factories first built here by the British).*

113 *Shanghai is the largest city in China and also the most westernized. Between the mid-19th century and the advent of the People's Republic of China, the Europeans made Shanghai a spearhead of their colonial policy. As a "bridge" between China and the West, the city very quickly became a symbol of colonial power worldwide. From an architectural standpoint there are still many signs of its recent past, as this panoramic view of the Zhongshan Lu - or Bund - clearly shows.*

114-115 *The Nanjing Lu, or Nanking Road, Shanghai's main shopping street, is certainly on a par with the Wangfujing in Beijing or Nathan Road in Hong Kong. Its bright lights are the new symbol of a city in the throes of rapid change.*

115 top *In Shanghai, as in every other modern city, the rush hour means traffic chaos but here, unlike elsewhere, the roads are still crowded with bicycles.*

115 bottom *Nowhere else in China do shops do as much business - and offer such a wide range of products - as in Shanghai. In the last few years big department stores, like the Shanghai Orient Shopping Centre, have opened in the city centre.*

116 *Bicycles - "zixingche" in Chinese - are still the most common means of transport in China, although the number of motorbikes and private cars on the roads is constantly increasing.*

117 *The Peace Hotel, or "Heping Fandian", is a symbol of colonial architecture in Shanghai. Built in 1906, it was frequented by businessmen and bankers, politicians, writers and artists; nowadays many foreign tourists stay there. Besides its glorious past, of which there is still extensive evidence, it has an enviable position, on the crossroads of the Nanjing Lu and Zhongshan Lu, right on the waterfront of the river Huang-p'u.*

118 *The ancient art of tai chi is popular all over China: groups of enthusiasts exercise in front of the Shanghai Mansions, one of the city's best hotels.*

119 top *A master of jujitzu instructs a very young novice in a street in central Shanghai.*

119 bottom *Every morning, before going to work in factories or offices, large groups of people gather to go through traditional gymnastics routines together. Here, a group of women on Shanghai's Bund perform exercises using a sword.*

120-121 *In The mornings there are unusual sights to see on the Bund: a Western folk dance is being performed by this group in a large open space, just yards away from the busy traffic of the city centre.*

The old Chinese city

122 top *The Temple of the Jade Buddha is definitely the foremost Buddhist temple in Shanghai: the precious white jade statue of the "Enlightened One" conserved here is an object of pilgrimage, and many believers come every year to meditate and worship.*

122 bottom *The temple is cared for by the monks who hold regular religious services; a low-priced, unpretentious little restaurant provides pilgrims with sustenance in the form of simple, traditional Buddhist dishes.*

123 *The term "Buddha", often incorrectly used as a proper name, is actually an adjective meaning awakened or enlightened one. The last Buddha was Siddhartha Gautama who descended from a noble Indian family; at the age of 30, dissatisfied with his empty, dissolute existence, he renounced his riches and started to preach a new form of religious understanding.*

124-125 *Religious fitments and ornamentation and statues of Buddha and other Buddhist saints help create the mystic, solemn atmosphere typically found in places of worship of all the earth's religions.*

126-127 *In the heart of the Chinese city, not far from the "foreign concessions" district, the Wu Xing Ting tea pavilion stands on a platform at the centre of an artificial lake; this typically Chinese structure was once the home of a rich Mandarin.*

128 *The population of China is put at around 1,200 million. After the Communist Revolution of 1949, the rulers of the new China had many serious problems to face, the most urgent being the need to feed a growing mass of people. Today undernourishment and hunger are things of the past, distant but not forgotten.*